# A Dark Wood

*New Women's Voices Series, No. 187*

*poems by*

# Marianne Burke

*Finishing Line Press*
Georgetown, Kentucky

# A Dark Wood

ACKNOWLEDGMENTS

*The New Yorker:* "Hands," "Funeral Home," "Shirts," "Little Whaley, Pawling, NY,"
"Vigil," "Mrs. M.'s Dollhouse"
*The Threepenny Review:* "At the Palace of Fine Arts, San Francisco"
*Southwest Review:* "Astoria, Queens, NY"
*Poetry:* "A Flute Overheard"
*Southern Poetry Review:* "Starlings"
*Boulevard:* "Our Daily Bread"



Publisher: Leah Huete de Maines
Editor: Christen Kincaid
Cover Art: *Hellebore*, by Eric Lindbloom
Author Photo: Donna Burke
Cover Design: Elizabeth Maines McCleavy


Order online: www.finishinglinepress.com
also available on amazon.com

Author inquiries and mail orders:
Finishing Line Press
PO Box 1626
Georgetown, Kentucky 40324
USA

# Contents

A Dark Wood, 1946.................................................................1

Vigil ........................................................................................2

Hands .....................................................................................4

Shirts ......................................................................................5

Little Whaley, Pawling, NY .................................................6

My Brother's Scar.................................................................9

Astoria, Queens, NY .........................................................10

Our Daily Bread..................................................................12

Mrs. M's Dollhouse ...........................................................13

Family Photo, 1977.............................................................15

Starlings ...............................................................................17

At the Palace of Fine Arts, San Francisco......................18

A Flute Overhead ...............................................................19

Love Poem ...........................................................................20

Youth Dew, My Mother's Perfume ..................................21

Funeral Home .....................................................................23

Golden Age...........................................................................24

Mother-In-Law ...................................................................25

Bethany Beach .....................................................................26

March ....................................................................................27

Insomnia...............................................................................28

Treehouse..............................................................................29

With Emily in the Woods...................................................30

Driving to Canaan Meeting House for a Poetry Reading .....31

Lost Election, 2024..............................................................32

Solar Eclipse ........................................................................33

Indian Lake Road, Millerton, NY....................................34

# A Dark Wood, 1946

Evergreens the color of lake water, depthless,
dark. It all comes back—these woods familiar
as a jacket worn in the elbows, sleeves.
I'd roam for hours below the mountain's
hard face, its crags spotted with pitch pine,
jump across rocks and streams, graceful

as a deer, even with a rifle in my hand.
He's gone hunting they'd think, it gave me
an excuse. Only occasionally I'd shoot,
hating how the sound assaulted the air, ruined
the silence I loved. These deer my brothers and
sisters, the mirror of God St. Francis said.

I looked for signs—antler rubs, peeled bark
off trees, fresh dirt on the forest floor cleared
of leaves and duff, a dominate buck's territory.
In war's onslaught we fought, animals
convulsed with fear, scraping in blood and
excrement, a charged metallic smell in the air.

I dream of deer, hear them chewing apples
in our yard, their breath, snorts of puffed air.
Spooked, white tails up, they retreat
into no man's land where I wait in a foxhole
watching men die, the silence broken by animal
grunts, haunted by my own breathing.

## Vigil

Nights, I stood in the bedroom window,
a target for eyes,
camouflaged by trees.

The aboveground pool, swing set,
clothesline—our daylight
yard—became extinct.

Then it was yours, your private
woods, where you'd sit,
far from the house,

under close-knit branches,
drinking beer, and burning holes
in the dark with cigarettes.

I saw each eye
grow red, redder
as you inhaled.

Sometimes I'd approach,
offer you another beer,
wait for "Yes" or "No,"

my father's voice,
to come from the smoke.
You disappeared

in fur-lined dark,
a possum, with night
eyes keeping watch.

I hoped you'd see me,
daughter, co-conspirator—
I knew you were a stranger,

that you preferred to live
outside, in a ragged nest
of leaves.

Was it cunning or dumb
luck that made you succeed,
disappear for good?

In one shot
you ruptured the heart
of the animal you'd become

during those long nights
of rehearsals, playing
dead, shut in the back yard,

your coffin.
No trick can make you
reappear, walk back

up the cellar stairs,
paper in hand, ready
for coffee, a cigarette,

grateful for my mother's
morning face, scarred
with sleep, waiting

on the other side
of the kitchen table,
where you'd sit

shaking yourself
from this bad dream.
Maybe it was fear—

I know the smell,
acrid, sweaty.
Today a fox has left it,

with his wild signature
tracked outside,
in snow, behind the house.

## Hands

Unadorned, they sat in our kitchen,
limp from the press of my mother's fingers.
All day she stood behind pedestals
of shoulders. I'd watch her
stand over them—elbows bent, arms
pumping lather. Eyes closed,
they willingly handed over their heads.
Hair was the one thing they could change.
In curlers they looked electric, pink.

Sometimes my mother was my customer.
The brush I held plowed its teeth
through her hair, turning the dark roots,
the magic oils that made it grow.
Silently, I counted the strokes, waiting
for her to give up, lean
her head back into my expert hands.

A helpless customer, I pay strangers
to turn my hair light, lighter.
Soon I won't remember its original color.
If I could I'd go on counting the strokes,
backward this time.
In the middle of our kitchen I'd tell you
it's no use
orphaned from your powerful, mothering hands.

## Shirts

*Is there anything cleaner than a clean white shirt?*
—Octavio Paz

There was no poetry waiting for my mother
in the week's worth of shirts.
Her arm would have to travel a long way,
steering the small boat of the iron
on a slow, repetitive journey up
and down the backs of my father's shirts,
the narrow channels of his sleeves,
while "As the World Turns" was on the TV.
She never asked for help, though I wanted
to give it; instead she ordered me
outside to play, saying I'd have to
do this work soon enough someday—
she didn't want a mother's little helper.
I'm grateful to her for that, and for
other freedoms she was never granted, like
sleeping with a man who is not your husband.
This morning, I watch from bed as you iron
your white shirt, pleased that such
an important thing as women's work
does not come between us.

## Little Whaley, Pawling, NY

*Sky Watch*

In this book, the stars are well connected,
dot to dot their bodies take shape,

crowding the black circle of heaven.
When we turn from flashlit page to sky,

they become harder to identify,
like trying to find Venus

in a diagram of the female anatomy—
the clitoris, a planet rarely seen,

never stands hoodless, bared.
That smear must be the Milky Way.

When you point out Big and Little Dippers,
I see our metal one dripping

from the tub of rainwater.
The stars above the lake are not set

neat as pins but spilled by the drunk
god who said, "To hell with the moon."

We drift in the canoe, folded
into the dark, our faces extinguished.

*Emptying the Chamber Pot*

Alone in Llewoh, in one of a handful
of cabins (circa 1906) scattered

around the lake, we slept deeper,
animals hibernating, pressed

together for warmth. I stirred once
to squat over the pot,

my sudden stream hitting bottom
broke the seal of quiet.

In the morning, you kindly offer,
but it's mine—this piss pool,

stagnant, in the white chamber pot.
I carry it, steady, down the stairs.

Piss proud, I walk out of the kitchen,
thick with its coffee smell,

and before I toss it from the rock
the summer occupants have marked

I admire, once more, its color—
the bronzed yellow of fallen leaves.

*Little Whaley*

It's warm for October, like spring.
As you row, I talk about the lake—

how like a clear mind it seems,
unshakeable even when trees shake at fever

pitch, scarlet and yellow, on its surface.
Underwater, a forest—leafy, gorgeous—

thrives, slowly sucking the lake dry.

You start to undress.
Flushed, I point to what's left

of our cabin, a blue stamp,
foreign, on the hillside,

at the blue heron,
how it flares from the trees,

a silent alarm.

I use my eyes, taking you
slowly, avoiding your greedy

stare, to press you deeper
under the glass of memory—

hard against this paradise
leafed in flame.

## My Brother's Scar

Some calls aren't even close, like when
the tumor they said was benign wasn't.
Never mind how this could happen to you.
Now the rotten part of your lung is gone.
Below your shoulder blade it looks as though
a giant compass planted one foot, and with
the other slowly traced a half circle.
I see the transfiguring scar, how it mimics
the arc of an angel's arm in a baroque painting.
Robust, it reaches upward, extending the arc
with trumpet raised. The sky's pitch dark;
it's the day to end all days. That arm, all ivory,
in the painting's heady gloom astonishes.
Once again the angels win and your scar,
its sideways crazy smile, declares you saved.

**Astoria, Queens, NY**

*Blue*

   Here, the Old World still thrives—
Mediterranean, with grape arbors, vines
curling like hair on trellis fences

in the back alleyways. Bowers,
really, with fig trees and flowering
squash. In some front gardens, chickens.

And Virgins, too, the inside shells
of their grottos immaculate, blue.
Ground is precious, packed with

hives of row houses, families woven
tight, sturdy as brick. Salvia and
cosmos displayed—bright, celebratory

flags in front gardens, where scarved
widows sit, their stares poison
to outsiders like us. Still,

there's hope in the sky-colored
tabletops of the neighborhood cafe.
In the mirrored walls everything's

clear at once, the back of your head,
your face. With elbows dug in,
we lean across the tidy blue square,

talking. Think of the emptied
swimming pool in Astoria Park, how
well tended, even in mid-September—

an open vault, big enough
for Astoria's extended families,
painted fresh in aquamarine.

*Hell Gate*

    More like an ancient viaduct than
a railroad bridge, Hell Gate presides
over Astoria, familiar and remote,

a monument, especially at dusk
as light gathers behind it—
a bas-relief, electrified.

Anywhere's within its reach.
To live here is to be locked in,
overshadowed by arches towering

godlike over everyone,

like this family. All figurines,
they've set up long folding tables
in the park, with Hell Gate near.

Too near. What if the bridge collapses
in some violent act of nature?
Just the thing that happens

at these sorts of get-together.
A dog lifts its leg on a baby carriage;
the mother screams. The worst passes.

**Our Daily Bread**

Below the bakery
loaves ripen in the dark,
the smell of their making
meets me in the street,
and we walk along together.

Let me tell you about bread,
and here it turns out its pockets
emptying more of its smell in the air,
there's never enough.
We perish before we are eaten.
At night they remove us from the shelves,
careful not to give people ideas.
Make the store look out of business,
make it say, there's no more here.

Think of Diamond Row
after the merchants have stripped
the velvet necks of their
diamonds and gold.
They're crazy
to think they've removed
all temptation.

## Mrs. M.'s Dollhouse

She's returned to her first
house, a replica her grandfather
built. The number plate's

been polished; the same No. 54,
a brass charm fastened to the door.
On the newel post, her mother's

perfume cap, circa 1932.
Her daughter and I used to play
here, like birds we filled

the empty rooms with scraps.
Today, credenzas, lyre-back
chairs, tilt-top tables

of mahogany, cherry wood.
Chandeliers, the size
of costume earrings.

And formal dinnerware
she sets with tweezers.
Never again will she say,

"I can't have anything."
The flower painting above
the mantel hides a built-in

safe, inside are thumbnail
tens and twenties. Upstairs,
in the master bedroom, a pair

of slippers, in an armchair
knitting left unfinished, as
if she expected her parents

any minute. This is how
it might have been—
her room next to theirs,

frosted pink, the skirted bed,
a cake made every day for her,
Mother's favorite baby doll.

## Family Photo, 1977

A lifetime has passed
since that photograph, lost now,
except when I go back to it,

unbury you from the cold
and snow we laid you in. Strange
to think I'm older than you were

that Christmas, our last one together.
Strange, too, that somewhere
this photo still exists. We're

frozen in place—you're squatting,
a hunting dog between your knees,
mother in a red dress, hair freshly

done, looking brave. Unlike my brothers
and me who do not smile, she dared
the camera to show the truth—

father's not himself. That explains
your hang-dog look—you were not
the father we knew but an alien one

caught like prey in a hunter's trap.
You never said a word. Yet you must've
welcomed your shadow,

an open grave in which to disappear.
The certificate recorded cause of death:
self-inflicted gunshot wound.

Your depression's a mystery, cloudy
like my memory of that January day.
I ran barefoot for help, away

from my mother's screams. Afterwards,
our silence fell like snow—
Years have piled up, so much

unfinished business as if
a door between the living and
the dead is left ajar.

**Starlings**
*(for my brother)*

Summers the train staggers
into the light at 125th.

A fire hydrant is blowing; children
spring in and out of the blast,

arms flailing. Starlings, I think,
the ones I'd watch outside my window

bathing, dipping beaks first, full
of starling joy, shaking themselves

silly in the gutter.
I recall how we tested

the wings of our arms
in the backyard pool.

How the water we threw
at the sky fell in crystal

drops crowning our heads.
Today your son and daughter,

the newest of starlings,
stand in wet bathing suits

holding hands for the camera.
In the chilled air their ribs expand.

Unfledged,
except for the hair

on their heads
matted, slick as afterbirth.

## At the Palace of Fine Arts, San Francisco

A grove of columns on the lawn—
their tinge the pink of frescoed

ceilings depicting the moment
when God's arm breaks

open the sky and light
pours like rain—

wavers now on the pond
ready to collapse

at the slightest disturbance:
the rote movements of two swans.

At the top of each column—women,
colossal, stricken in postures of indolence.

Green and white strands of pigeon dung
fall to their shoulders.

Homeless among these women who keep
their backs turned against the living,

a man sits grooming himself
as if he, too, were a god.

His mirror an oracle,
he moves slowly before his face.

## A Flute Overheard

I feel its weight,

the way you will yourself

to carry it uphill

night after night.

I note the long

pauses, the gravity

of your exertions

this early spring

when the air

overripe with jasmine

promises

something other than

this solitary life.

## Love Poem

At this early hour there's clarity,
the sweet blend of birds,
their song a steady stream
I drink in.  Notes rise, fall.
Some are visible— starlings
on the roof, the yellow dips of
finches.  A crow caws the air,
its wing flap a brief disturbance,
the shadow of an unpleasant thought.

No words, but sounds like scraps
of this and that, something a bird
might use to build its nest.
Where you are it is evening, and
the silence between us is unnatural—
the different hemispheres we inhabit
separate cages— our voices cannot
chatter about everyday things.

Now with your return days away,
your remembered voice
reaches the strand of this new day.
Our silence will soon break—
words rushing in a brook, babbling
over old, familiar stones.

## Youth Dew, My Mother's Perfume

A lost smell,
heavy as incense
shaken about the altar.
The priest a cloud of smoky
breath. This Sunday holiness
brought me to attention.

Thou shalt, thou shalt not
the voice of my mother,
the god in our house
who brought me
to worldly attention
on those rare nights out
when she stood before
the mirror holding up
a necklace for me to clasp,
letting me pull the zipper
of her dress closed.
Hips and waist defined,
the shock of her body.

*Holy, holy, holy*

This new self
anointed with Youth
Dew, her smell the musk
of it on her throat,
overpowering the room
like a third presence,
the body waking.

It's safe now to think
of them as lovers, godless
in their desire.
Imagine her in nothing
but that perfume, my
father losing himself
inside of her, another
kind of worship.

*Only say the word*

The word is beautiful
in body and soul,
imperishable,
even though the world
is empty of her.
There is no word, now,
only sometimes
this nighttime smell.

## Funeral Home

Let us think of you spared, carried gently
in the arms of the ocean that's piped
through speakers, spreading a hush in Parmele's,
where we sit, adrift, on the parlor couch
between time, in death's caesura.

The funeral director ticks off a list
of questions. He wants the facts, reduces you
to an abstract—mother with a capital "M."
Nowhere will it say how petite you were,
that your wedding ring fits my pinkie finger,

or that, tucked into your coffin, you will look
like a doll we will never outgrow.
Downstairs, he shows us his fleet
of caskets, satin-lined, open-lidded—
music boxes whose strains are too fine

for us to hear, like your voice,
utterless, our names dead on your tongue.
Even here the ocean's cold hush.

You are lost at sea.
To think we must choose a vessel,
one that will not float but sink.
Mahogany is what we set you in—
our mother of pearl, our buried treasure.

## Golden Age
*(for Margaret Hollister, 1917-2019)*

Nearing ninety, you retrace your steps

to that other China—Peking, your first home,
imperial in its own right, you the daughter
of God, the child of missionaries.

That China had two faces—western,
its church towers folded hands pointed
toward the empire to come; the other,

eastern, single storied yellow and red temples,
palaces haunted by ancestor spirits who
preferred this world, as imperfect as it is.

Your itinerary's a trail of storybook places—
Forbidden City, Temple of Heaven,
Sacred Way.  Even natural disasters,

the earthquake of 1921, have lost their terror,
become yet another story of how the mountains
walked and the dragon beneath them twitched its tail.

This ancient China blossoms again,
a paradise untouched by God. Here the past is golden,
honey sweet, not bitter.  In its afterglow you see yourself

at the Summer Palace with the lover
your father forbade you to meet, walking arm in arm
into another life, the one you never lived.

## Mother-In-Law

Our stations in life turned. I'm the elder and she,
nearing one hundred, the child naked in the tub.
Leaning back legs outstretched, she's free to float
above the body's aches and pains. She paddles water
with ancient hands, laughs at the splashes she creates.
It's disarming to hear her chortle like a little girl as if
she were one of her great granddaughters. Her flesh
is chicken skin hanging loose, the large breasts
empty sacks flat against her chest. She calls a balled knot
on the back of her skull a wisdom bump. So be it. Her iron
will has lost its strength. She's in my hands now, waits
for me to pour water over her gray, thinning crown.

## Bethany Beach

Human voices surround me
yet all I hear is ocean,
the long sweep of its reach.
There's privacy, even on
this crowded beach, to lose
oneself. Egoless, I drift—
loose seaweed in the current.

Here is where we returned you
that February when we cast
your ashes into the ocean's
bodiless depths—to a world
beyond this one, immaterial,
our names, like yours,
*writ in Water.*

The ocean swells in waves
of muscle to pound its weight
on shore. Sand shifts beneath
my feet. A sandpiper edges close
with mock derring-do then skitters
away from the surf's dying hiss.

# March

*Our life is March weather, savage and serene in one hour*
—Ralph Waldo Emerson

My cat, mad for contact, stretches toward me,
his fur warm under my hand as if he'd been
lying by a fire instead of this late winter sun.
Eyes closed, I face the warmth, feel the pleasure
it brings knowing it's only one day in this month
of false springs. Tomorrow could bring snow.
Something in me holds on to winter, wants to
stay dormant under sodden leaves, then look up
at a new sun, revived. It's the lengthening days,
the springing forward toward decline
that give me pause—the spots on the back
of my hands and forearms tell of aging
as does the lichen blistering on leafless trees.

## Insomnia

Your breathing's caught
in your throat as if you were
climbing a mountain in your sleep.
I listen for a pause. Outside autumn
crickets hum, keep me company.
I wait for you to exhale—all
our married years past and ahead.

Now what? Begin again.
Remember jumping rope—how
I used to wait for the rope to hit
the ground before I leapt, feeling
the rhythm and swing of it.
My heart joins in, vibrates
in one ear against the pillow.

My blood's turbulent tonight.
Our bed that field long ago
where I lay summer nights
loving a boy the grass damp
beneath us, our bodies still green,
blundering into each other—
the crickets going wild.

## Treehouse

From my desk I've watched him
months now building a treehouse
from scratch.  He never tires
of climbing up and down
the ladder to saw, hammer, drill.
At times I hear him talk to himself,
a habit that usually annoys me, though
I can see he's on to something—
maybe a new idea, a problem solved.

I worry about the sugar maple, will it
survive caged in wood scaffolding,
nails driven into its limbs, wonder
how many years the girls will play
in this house their grandfather built
ten feet off the ground. Inside there's
a bucket sink connected to the garden
hose, a handmade drop-down table.
Heraldic red paint and thrift shop
drawer pulls trim the outside.

The girls have put up a welcome sign,
opened a restaurant—leaf soup, mud pies.
As yet there's no roof or second story,
but he's not done, continues runs to Home
Depot, adds more flooring, secures joints,
railings. He's busy, busy as a squirrel, an old
gray one, preparing for winter.

## With Emily in the Woods

Just when
we thought
we'd lost her
she reappears.
Her yellow shirt,
a bright spot
we follow—her eight-
year-old back, strong,
legs long, swift.
She runs through
November's graveyard
of skeletal trees,
sure-footed
on trails pocked
with roots.
The same roots
slow us down.
For her it might
as well be summer.
This wild girl's
growing into
her body as a
tree grows, with
leaves quickening,
green and new.
It's hard to look
back, see ourselves
at her age.
There's only
so much light
before the aperture
closes. We fall
further behind.
She runs toward
something
we cannot see.
Left in the past,
we kick up squalls
of old leaves.

**Driving to Canaan Meeting House for a Poetry Reading**

This summer evening the way clouds pile up
like sheep over Cardigan Mountain and the trees
and fields of tall grass turn gold in the sinking sun,
I could be driving through a nineteenth century landscape
by an old Master, a plein air painting of the New England
countryside. Imagine catching such light, like painting air
or the atmosphere before everything shifts
and what you're looking at is no longer there, only fool's gold—
a rusted tractor, weeds up to its back axles, an abandoned farm,
the family name barely legible on the barn, a Dollar General,
signs for CBD oil, the Abundant Life Church of God.
Up ahead some self-appointed guardian of geese made three
handwritten signs: Slow Down, Save Lives (recall roadside
memorials to loved ones killed in car crashes), the last one reads
Geese Crossing. Sure enough they appear, stop traffic, such as it is,
outside Canaan, NH. Soon they'll fly south sounding summer's end.
Not the goose I remember from Upton Lake that somehow
survived last winter, rejected by his kind, grounded for life
with only one wing. I tell myself there are worse things.

**Lost Election, 2024**

My granddaughters draw the continents
all seven on the asphalt in chalk purple
green blue—Earth spread flat before them.

The continents float noncontiguous,
free shapes with room to sprawl and grow.
Within these empty borders are the names

for each, in uneven imperfect script.
They leave the oceans nameless
fill the blanks with chalk hearts, happy faces—

theirs a world of benevolence.
Soon their handiwork will disappear
in weather, rain. November's come

and with it change, our world is drizzly, grim,
worse than a child's nightmare my dread
of what's to come, no map for where we are—

lost between a hawk and a buzzard.

## Solar Eclipse

This visitation from the heavens turned us
into believers. We came to the mountain
to see for ourselves. And it was so.
A thing strange: the moon at first a spot
in the eye of the sun. Our dark glasses helped
us see. We looked blind staring at the sky
like an audience at a 1950s movie waiting
for the creature of the black lagoon.
A chill descended. It grew dark, but sickly so—
the edges of buildings, trees tinted yellow.
The moon a boulder entombed the sun.
The atmosphere shadowy, bruised. We saw
darkly things that may or may not be true.
Then it was over, car taillights, a seam of red
coals burned a trail south on the interstate.

## Indian Lake Road, Millerton, NY

*Morning First Day*

Sun lights the back pasture as if a switch
were turned on. All that gray, a scrim

of fog rain has lifted, cleared away.
Across the lawn a swath of grass

lit day-glo green shines like water.
Trees, silver-wet, quicken in the wind,

the sky swept empty, a blue, cloudless room.
On a bed of flagstone, dogs sleep, the soft

engine of their breath, its in and out, an eddy
in an invisible stream of air where

birds build cathedrals of sound.
Not until a rooster crows do the dogs bark,

nuzzle my hand, *Come on, Come on.*
Still wet, expectant with light, this day begins.

*Dawn Second Day*

Outside, the world's morning face
has yet to materialize.  Half awake,

I cannot tell if what I'm seeing is beautiful or
sinister. Once (at twilight to be exact) stood

a fenced garden, pasture, trees, mountains.
At this ghost hour, fog has a life of its own,

a spirit one that hovers, hesitant to leave.
To walk out there would be to disappear,

to leave one life for the next. I should be
in bed, not standing at the window

in this somnolent, in-between state
but asleep like the dogs, who, thank God,

have not heard me. Or else I'd have to
let them out, only to call their names

into that dead space,
hoping they could hear me.

*Last Day*

Am I the divine master?
These dogs seem to think so.

Citronella candles on either side of me
waft smoke into the air, a kind of magic

that repels rather than attracts. Still
these two lie at my feet, content to wait.

What do the two hawks adrift, criss- crossing
in wide loops, or the hills far off, menthol-green,

mirage like, have to do with them?
After all, they have sat with me

through other mornings, other sunsets,
models of patience, leaving me

to wonder at this garden of plenty.

**Marianne Burke** taught English and creative writing at Montclair Kimberley Academy, an independent day school in Montclair, NJ, for over twenty years. Previously she worked in New York City at *The New Yorker* magazine and Sarah Lazin Books, a literary agency. She has held writing fellowships at Yaddo, MacDowell, and the Virginia Center for the Creative Arts. Her poems have appeared in *Southern Poetry Review, The New Yorker, Poetry, Southwest Review, The Threepenny Review, Boulevard,* and *Passages North.* She now lives in the Upper Valley of central New Hampshire.

www.ingramcontent.com/pod-product-compliance
Lightning Source LLC
Chambersburg PA
CBHW020219090426
42734CB00008B/1131